NATIONAL
GEOGRAPHIC
KIDS

weird but true! 5

350 OUTRAGEOUS FACTS

NATIONAL GEOGRAPHIC
WASHINGTON, D.C.

THAT'S WEIRD!

A T. REX'S ARMS WERE SO SHORT, IT COULDN'T SCRATCH ITS NOSE!

5

The world's biggest **skateboard** is almost as long as a school bus!

DOCTORS
HAVE CREATED
HEART MUSCLE
FROM
HUMAN
SKIN.

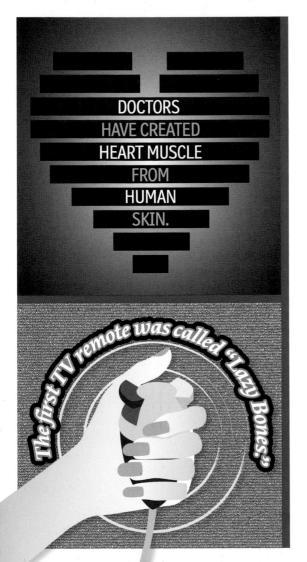
The first TV remote was called "Lazy Bones."

You can use Gatorade to clean your toilet.

A man once blew a bubble gum bubble that was larger than a basketball.

There's more salt in one gallon of seawater (3.79 L) than in 49 pounds (22.2 kg) of potato chips!

A GROUP
OF HIPPOS
IS SOMETIMES
CALLED A
BLOAT.

A **VENDING MACHINE** IN SINGAPORE **GAVE AWAY A FREE SODA** TO ANYONE WHO **HUGGED** THE MACHINE.

Giraffe hooves are the size of dinner plates.

ALL OF THE LETTERS IN THE WORD "TYPEWRITER"

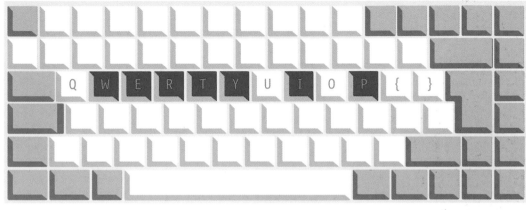

CAN BE FOUND IN ONE ROW ON A KEYBOARD.

HOT WATER CAN FREEZE FASTER THAN COLD WATER.

Sea snail mucus was once used to make purple dye.

The **first cars** didn't have windshield **wipers.**

CLOCKS WERE ONCE MADE WITH ONLY ONE HAND.

XII I II III IV V VI VII VIII IX X XI

SHARKS
CAN'T BLINK.

A GERMAN **FASHION** DESIGNER MADE **CLOTHING** FROM **MILK POWDER.**

GOATS SNACK ON **POISON IVY.**

A 35-FOOT-TALL, (10.7-m) INFLATED **ANGRY BIRD** PERCHED ON THE SIDE OF THE SEATTLE SPACE NEEDLE IN WASHINGTON STATE, U.S.A.

Ostriches can swim but they can't fly.

A U.S. ice-cream shop sold insect-flavored ice cream.

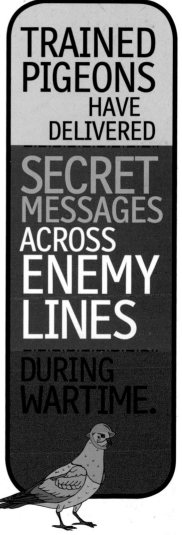

TRAINED PIGEONS HAVE DELIVERED SECRET MESSAGES ACROSS ENEMY LINES DURING WARTIME.

Sticking **raw bacon** in your **nostrils** can stop serious **nosebleeds.**

MALE TURKEYS ARE CALLED
GOBBLERS.

BEES HAVE FIVE EYES.

SOME BLUEBERRIES ARE **PINK.**

THERE ARE
180,000 ISLANDS

IN FINLAND—

THAT'S ONE FOR ABOUT
EVERY 30 PEOPLE
IN THE COUNTRY.

IN TAIWAN, GARBAGE TRUCKS BLAST MUSIC TO REMIND PEOPLE TO BRING OUT THE TRASH.

Some crabs are bright purple.

SOME ANTS LICK
EACH OTHER TO PROTECT AGAINST DISEASES.

Water blown out of a blue whale's spout can shoot three stories high.

SOME **POLICE OFFICERS** IN CAIRO, EGYPT, PATROL THE **PYRAMIDS** ON **CAMELBACK.**

25

Spider **silk** is used to make **fishing nets** in some countries.

Raindrops are shaped like hamburger buns.

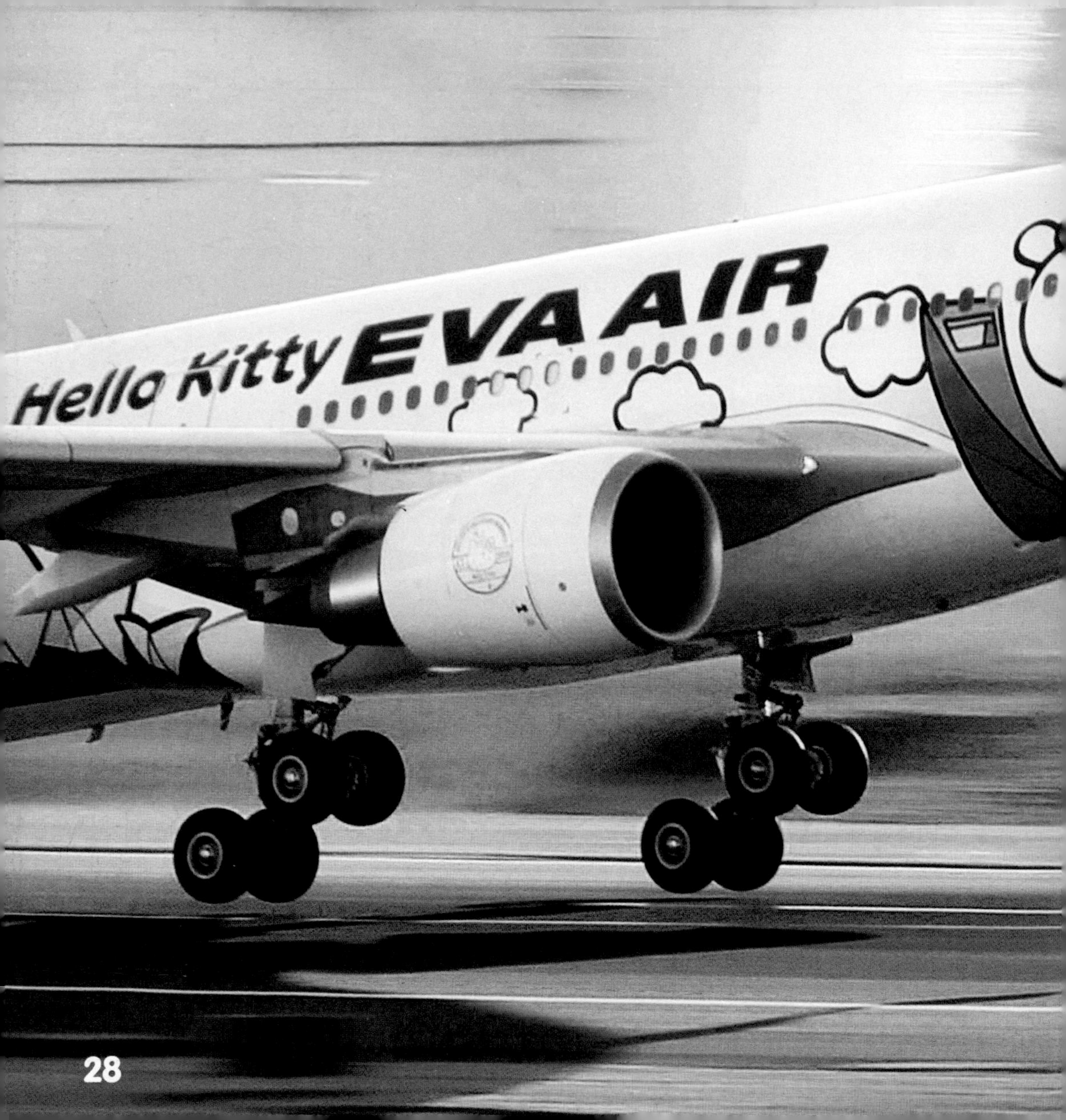
Hello Kitty
EVA AIR

A Taiwanese airline flies Hello Kitty-themed jets.

Triceratops **had up to 800 teeth.**

WHEN IT GETS COLD ENOUGH,
NIAGARA FALLS—
ONE OF THE
LARGEST WATERFALLS
IN NORTH AMERICA—
CAN FREEZE OVER.

Some wildflowers smell like chocolate.

A CANADIAN WOMAN
RODE A MOTORIZED TOILET
UP TO 46 MILES AN HOUR!

(74 km/h)

R.I.P.

RETIRED
BEN AND JERRY'S
ICE-CREAM
FLAVORS ARE LAID
TO REST AT THE
FLAVOR
GRAVEYARD
IN VERMONT, U.S.A.

Insect blood can be **clear, yellow, or green.**

IT CAN BE MORE
SATISFYING
TO SCRATCH AN
ITCH
ON YOUR BACK
THAN ON YOUR ARM.

THERE'S A HORSE THAT'S SO SMALL SHE SLEEPS IN A DOGHOUSE.

Kinkajous can twist their hind feet **backward** to climb trees.

36

YOU WOULD WEIGH **ZERO POUNDS** AT THE CENTER OF (0 kg)

EARTH.

A Welshman's **dog** served as **best man** at his wedding.

IF YOUR TONGUE WAS AS LONG AS A FROG'S, IT WOULD REACH DOWN TO YOUR BELLY BUTTON!

A candy company makes **gummy bears** the size of **footballs.**

SUNSETS

SAUCE CAN MAKE
TABASCO
BEE STINGS HURT LESS.

ON MARS ARE BLUE.

Saltwater taffy does not contain saltwater.

THERE'S A MILLIPEDE THAT HAS 750 LEGS.

FULL MOONS APPEAR BRIGHTER IN WINTER THAN IN SUMMER.

MORE PEOPLE HAVE BEEN TO **THE MOON** THAN TO THE BOTTOM OF THE OCEAN.

SOME BONOBOS USE TOUCH-SCREEN COMPUTERS TO COMMUNICATE WITH HUMANS.

Turtles the size of small cars roamed Earth 60 million years ago.

A leech can suck up five times its body weight in blood.

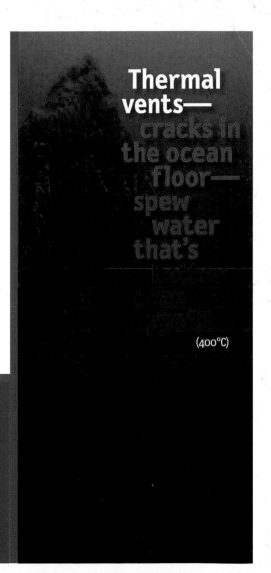

Thermal vents— cracks in the ocean floor— spew water that's hotter than 750°F (400°C)

FORMULA 1 DRIVERS have to REMOVE the STEERING WHEEL **TO GET IN AND OUT OF THEIR CARS.**

SAFFRON is the world's most **EXPENSIVE SPICE,** selling for up to **$16 A GRAM** (.04 oz).

GIANT PUMPKINS can grow as much as **50 POUNDS** (23 kg) **A DAY.**

WORKERS sometimes **RAPPEL DOWN** the **WASHINGTON MONUMENT** in Washington, D.C., U.S.A.

RYUGYONG HOTEL in Pyongyang, North Korea, has been under construction for **30 YEARS,** but has **NEVER OFFICIALLY OPENED.**

Britain's **TALLEST UNBROKEN WATERFALL** is almost entirely **UNDERGROUND.**

U.S. president **HARRY TRUMAN** traveled in a **PLANE** nicknamed the **"SACRED COW."**

GECKOS LICK THEIR EYEBALLS **TO KEEP THEM CLEAN.**

An Italian chef **MAKES SUSHI** in the shape of **BASKETBALL SHOES.**

SCIENTISTS have built a **DATABASE** showing what **ANIMALS** are capable of **PASSING GAS.**

A Japanese company makes **SAMURAI ARMOR** FOR PETS.

That's Weird!

MEERKATS SLEEP ON TOP OF ONE ANOTHER IN A PILE.

Some people use **coffee grounds** to make their **hair shiny.**

Ping-Pong balls can travel (113 km/h) **70 miles an hour—** that's faster than a speeding car!

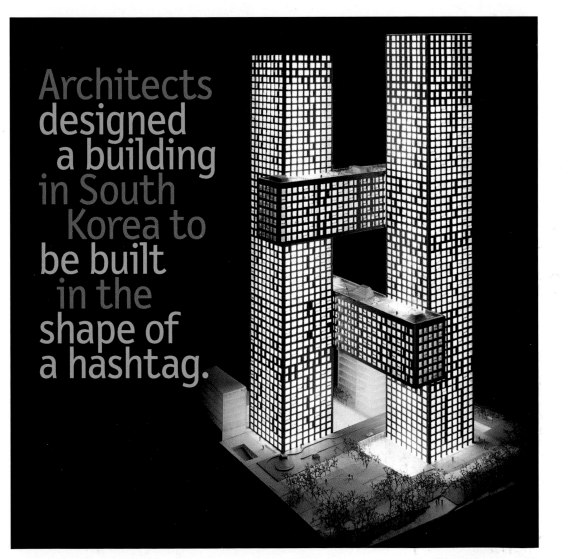

Architects designed a building in South Korea to be built in the shape of a hashtag.

THE STRONGEST TORNADOES ARE PACKED WITH ENOUGH ENERGY TO POWER 10,000 HOUSES FOR ONE DAY.

A WHITE ORCA WAS SPOTTED IN THE PACIFIC OCEAN.

SOME TARANTULAS ARE BLUE.

You can **buy a wig** for your dog.

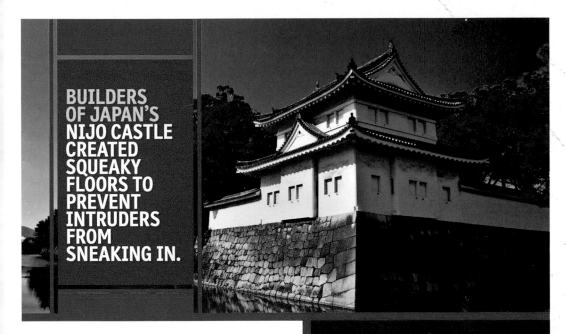

BUILDERS OF JAPAN'S NIJO CASTLE CREATED SQUEAKY FLOORS TO PREVENT INTRUDERS FROM SNEAKING IN.

A sea star can turn its stomach **inside Out.**

A baseball stadium in Texas, U.S.A., **sold hot dogs** that were each longer than **two iPads.**

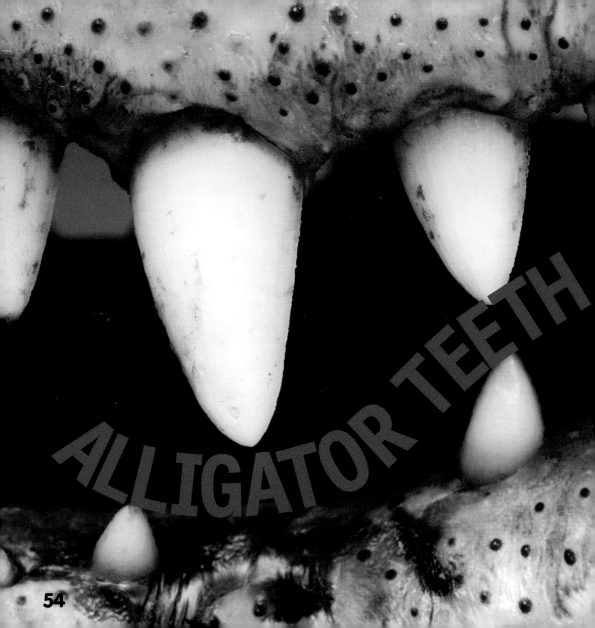

ALLIGATOR TEETH

ARE HOLLOW.

THE
**WORLD'S
LARGEST
BAT** HAS A
WINGSPAN
AS WIDE AS
A SOFA.

FINGERPRINTS CAN LAST FOR UP TO 40 YEARS ON PAPER.

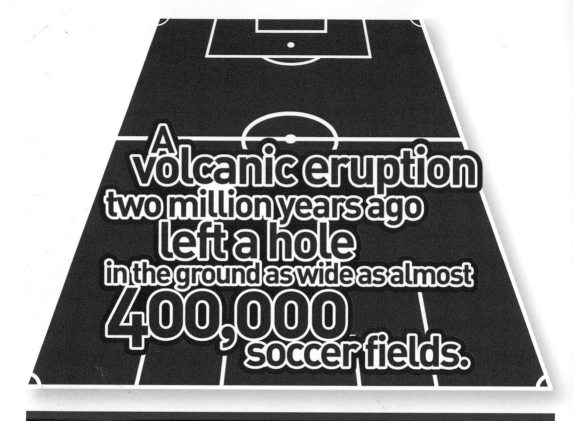

A **volcanic eruption** two million years ago **left a hole** in the ground as wide as almost **400,000** soccer fields.

YOU COULD COOK A LARGE PIZZA ON THE SURFACE OF **VENUS** IN **NINE SECONDS!**

Ladybugs might play **dead** when threatened.

A company in England created **cheese-scented perfume.**

Babies have taste buds in their cheeks.

Spaceship Earth
at Walt Disney
World Resort in
Florida, U.S.A.,
weighs as much as

17 jumbo jets.

Whales
have
belly buttons.

A prize **cow** in Canada sold for **1.2 million dollars.**

A **STUDY** FOUND THAT THE **MORE AFRAID** YOU ARE OF **SPIDERS,** THE **BIGGER** THEY APPEAR TO BE.

IN ANCIENT **EGYPT,** ONLY ROYALTY WERE ALLOWED **TO EAT** MUSHROOMS.

Some **people** are born with a double row of eyelashes.

12,345,678,

111,111,111
x111,111,111

987,654,321

Some ancient Romans paid their taxes in honey.

It was considered **good luck** to throw shoes at the bride and groom at 16th-century weddings **in England.**

A **hot drink** can sometimes **cool you down** faster than a **cold drink.**

BEAVERS HAVE A SET OF CLEAR EYELIDS TO SEE UNDERWATER.

UP UNTIL 100 YEARS AGO, SOME TOOTHBRUSH BRISTLES WERE MADE FROM PIG HAIRS.

SEAWEED CAN PREVENT TOOTH DECAY.

Fish sometimes cough.

OOLOGY IS THE STUDY OF **BIRD EGGS.**

A **pineapple** is actually made up of a **bunch of berries.**

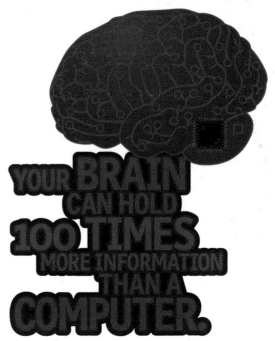

There's a **jellyfish** that can change from an adult back into a baby.

YOUR **BRAIN** CAN HOLD **100 TIMES** MORE INFORMATION THAN A **COMPUTER.**

THE ORIGINAL ARCHITECTS OF THE
GOLDEN GATE BRIDGE
IN SAN FRANCISCO, CALIFORNIA, U.S.A.,
CONSIDERED PAINTING THE BRIDGE
BLACK WITH
YELLOW STRIPES
INSTEAD OF ORANGE.

A MAN IN HAVANA, CUBA, BUILT A BICYCLE THAT'S AS TALL AS AN ELEPHANT!

Cockroaches recognize members of their family.

500 million tweets are sent every day.

There's a town in Oregon, U.S.A., named Boring.

A PARADE FLOAT WITH A GIANT BALLOON IS CALLED A FALLOON.

ACTUAL BUILDING IN DUBAI, UAE.

IT TOOK **450,300 LEGO BRICKS** TO CREATE AN **18-FOOT-TALL** REPLICA OF (5.5-m) **THE SKYSCRAPER BURJ KHALIFA!**

ASTRA

IS THE FEAR OF

PHOBIA

THUNDER AND LIGHTNING.

A chameleon's **tongue** can travel as fast as **13 miles** (21 km/h) an hour

An insect called an **assassin bug** sometimes carries dead ants on its back to appear bigger.

81

Three back-to-back **strikes** in bowling is called a **turkey.**

Elephants drink the equivalent of **800 glasses of water** a day.

Only female mosquitoes bite.

Whale blubber was once used to make margarine.

TWO-STORY BUILDING
AND CAN HOLD 75 KIDS.

The temperature of EXOPLANET KELT-9b reaches 7,820°F (4,327°C)— hotter than most stars!

NAKED MOLE RATS have evolved to FEEL ALMOST NO PAIN.

U.S. PRESIDENT WOODROW WILSON GOLFED in the SNOW using BLACK GOLF BALLS.

The surface area of the PACIFIC OCEAN is larger than that of all the CONTINENTS COMBINED.

EACH CENTURY, the length of a day on Earth GETS LONGER BY 1/500 OF A SECOND.

A 48-MILLION-YEAR-OLD "NESTING DOLL" FOSSIL SHOWS A SNAKE THAT ATE A LIZARD THAT ATE AN INSECT.

There is a world "PUN-OFF" CHAMPIONSHIP held in AUSTIN, TEXAS, U.S.A., EVERY YEAR.

A group of pugs is called a GRUMBLE.

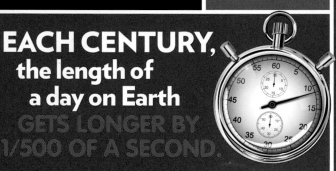

At the U.K.'s
SHETLAND PONY GRAND NATIONAL,
riders must be between
AGES 8 AND 13 and stand
SHORTER THAN FIVE FEET (1.5 m).

AVOLATTE = a latte served inside an avocado skin

CAPYBARAS—the largest rodents in the world—are used as therapy animals.

RESEARCHERS ARE STUDYING HOW **LADYBUGS FOLD THEIR WINGS** TO ONE DAY IMPROVE **UMBRELLA DESIGNS.**

That's Weird!

A jewelry store in Tokyo, Japan, sold a **24-KARAT-GOLD DARTH VADER** MASK.

CAMELS
ARE ORIGINALLY FROM
NORTH
AMERICA.

AMERICANS ARE MORE LIKELY TO **WIN A MILLION DOLLARS IN THE LOTTERY** THAN TO GET HIT BY **LIGHTNING.**

BABY EELS ARE CALLED **ELVERS.**

ON THE MOON YOU CAN THROW A BALL SIX TIMES FARTHER THAN YOU CAN ON EARTH.

An **octopus** can detach **an arm** on purpose and then **regrow it.**

The symbol **&**, which means **"and,"** was once a letter in the **English alphabet.**

You can buy **an energy bar with crickets** inside.

89

YOU CAN SEE A GLASS FROG'S HEART BEATING THROUGH **ITS SKIN.**

You will likely get

10,000

small cuts, bruises,

and sprains

in your lifetime.

A BUZZ LIGHTYEAR ACTION FIGURE SPENT 15 MONTHS ON THE INTERNATIONAL SPACE STATION.

93

An elephant's **heart** can weigh as much as a basset hound.

A LION'S **ROAR** IS LOUDER THAN A LAWN MOWER.

AGGRESSOR

YOU CAN TELL THE **PERSONALITY** OF SOME **FINCHES** BY THE **COLOR OF THEIR HEADS—** BIRDS WITH BLACK HEADS ARE RISK-TAKERS, WHILE REDHEADS ARE MORE AGGRESSIVE.

RISK-TAKER

In Japan you can buy octopus-flavored ice cream.

Some **millipedes** glow in the dark.

Orange snow once fell in Siberia.

300 MILLION YEARS AGO,
DRAGONFLIES
HAD
WINGSPANS
AS WIDE AS
THREE
FRISBEES.

Children in **ANCIENT ROME** played a game similar to **LEAPFROG.**

COLLEGE STUDENTS CREATED A PIANO OUT OF bananas.

EVERY DAY THERE ARE MORE **iPHONES** **SOLD** AROUND THE WORLD THAN THERE ARE **BABIES BORN.**

THE **PEACOCK MANTIS SHRIMP** HAS CLAWS STRONG ENOUGH TO **PUNCH** THROUGH AN AQUARIUM'S GLASS WALLS.

Doodling can help you concentrate

MORE THAN 100 YEARS AGO, PEOPLE ROLLER-SKATED

BY STRAPPING SMALL TIRES TO THEIR FEET.

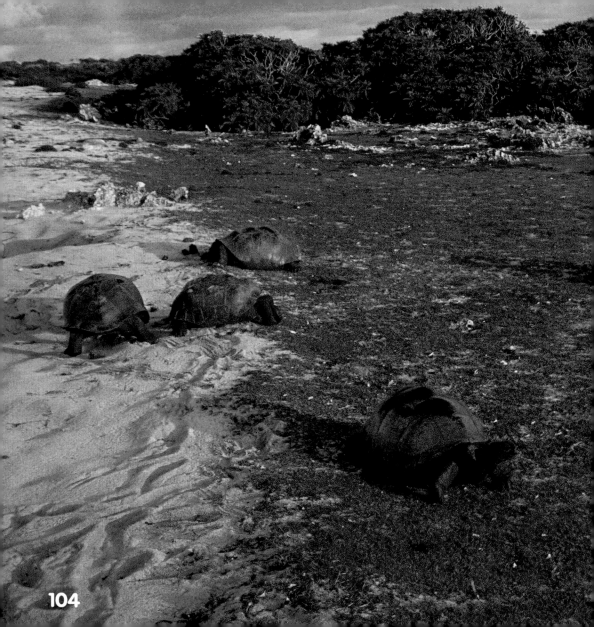

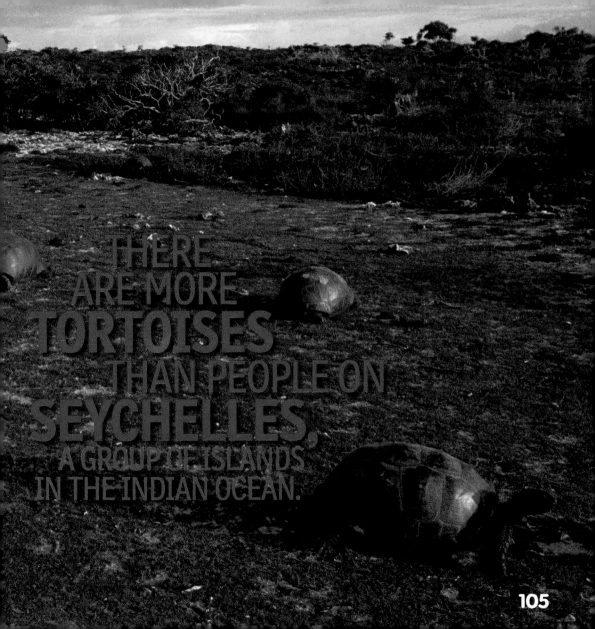

THERE ARE MORE **TORTOISES** THAN PEOPLE ON **SEYCHELLES,** A GROUP OF ISLANDS IN THE INDIAN OCEAN.

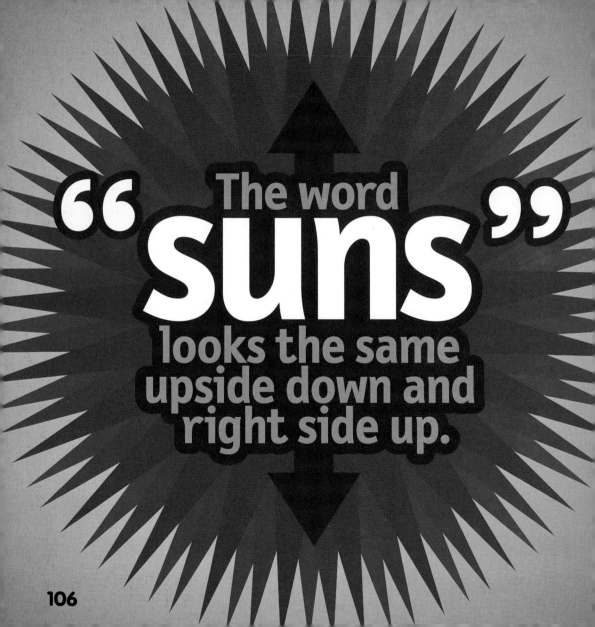

"The word **suns** looks the same upside down and right side up."

It's possible to use a **smart-phone** to turn off the lights.

Soup made from **birds' nests** is a Chinese delicacy.

A TURKISH MAN CAN SQUIRT MILK OUT OF HIS EYE, SHOOTING THE LIQUID OVER NINE FEET. (2.795 m)

107

LEGEND SAYS THAT PIRATE TREASURE MAY BE BURIED NEAR THE STATUE OF LIBERTY.

YOU CAN ORDER **FRIED** BONE MARROW FOR DINNER AT SOME FANCY RESTAURANTS.

THE U.S. POSTAL SERVICE **MAILS** MORE THAN **800,000** LIVE CHICKENS IN THE WEEKS LEADING UP TO EASTER.

Chili pepper crops grow **hotter** when there is less **rain.**

IT'S POSSIBLE FOR
A CROCODILE
TO EAT A SHARK.

SOME SPIDERS' BRAINS
EXTEND INTO THEIR LEGS.

BEAGLE + BOXER

BOGLE

THE INSIDE OF A **CUCUMBER** CAN BE UP TO **20°F COOLER** (11.1°C) THAN THE OUTSIDE AIR.

Your **lips** don't **sweat.**

CRACKERS ARE NAMED FOR THE CRACKLING SOUND THEY MAKE WHILE BAKING.

THE MWANZA flat-headed agama lizard resembles **SPIDER-MAN.**

One type of Australian orchid spends its entire life underground.

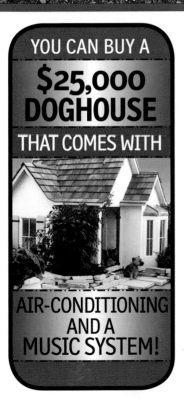

YOU CAN BUY A
$25,000 DOGHOUSE
THAT COMES WITH
AIR-CONDITIONING AND A MUSIC SYSTEM!

NIGHTTIME RAINBOWS ARE COMMON AT YOSEMITE NATIONAL PARK IN CALIFORNIA, U.S.A.

MOST **TORNADOES** OCCUR BETWEEN 3 p.m. AND 9 p.m.

A meteor crater in South Africa is wider than Ireland.

IT TOOK ABOUT **2.6 MILLION PEOPLE** TO BUILD

JAPAN'S TODAIJI TEMPLE IN THE EIGHTH CENTURY A.D.

A platypus **swims** with its ears and nostrils shut.

MELTING ICEBERGS CAN FLIP UPSIDE DOWN.

Fireflies can glow yellow, green, or orange.

A BOARD GAME WAS FOUND IN KING TUT'S TOMB.

SOME TUBE WORMS CAN LIVE FOR ABOUT **600 YEARS IN THE DEEP OCEAN.**

THE AUSTRALIAN **LYREBIRD** CAN MIMIC **CAR ALARMS.**

14 countries

sent just

ONE ATHLETE

to the

2016 Olympic Games.

An asteroid named **Vesta** is home to a **mountain** more than twice the size of Mount Everest.

BILLIONS OF YEARS AGO, EARTH REACHED **3,700°F.** (2,038°C) THAT'S SEVEN TIMES HOTTER THAN A BARBECUE GRILL AT A COOKOUT.

DIAPER DERBY = A RACE OF CRAWLING BABIES DURING HALFTIME AT U.S. PROFESSIONAL BASKETBALL GAMES

IF EARTH DIDN'T HAVE A MOON, IT WOULD SPIN SO FAST THAT A DAY WOULD LAST JUST SIX HOURS.

TREE-CLIMBING GOATS spread seeds by **SPITTING THEM.**

SCIENTISTS found evidence on a remote Siberian island that **humans first bred dogs to pull sleds.**

Some **NARWHALS** have **TWO TUSKS.**

CLIMATE CHANGE could make humans **TWICE AS SLEEP DEPRIVED,** a study found.

The **KING** of the **NETHERLANDS** sometimes works as a **COMMERCIAL AIRLINE PILOT.**

TABLE TENNIS WAS ONCE BANNED IN THE SOVIET UNION BECAUSE IT WAS BELIEVED THE GAME WAS HARMFUL TO THE EYES.

RESEARCHERS built a room so **SILENT** you can hear the grinding of your **BONES** as your **JOINTS MOVE.**

An artist created and hid **SIX "FORGOTTEN GIANTS" SCULPTURES** for explorers to find in **DENMARK.**

A newly discovered species of **GECKO** from **MADAGASCAR** has **detachable scales.**

A prehistoric relative of the **GUINEA PIG** was the size of a **COW.**

That's Weird!

About **235** different languages are spoken in China.

A GERMAN **MAN** DROVE ONE **CAR** **500,000** **MILES** (804,672 km) IN **23** YEARS.

THAT'S THE SAME DISTANCE AS DRIVING AROUND **THE GLOBE** **20 TIMES.**

All of the adults on Earth **weigh** a combined total of about **342** million tons.
(310 million metric tons)

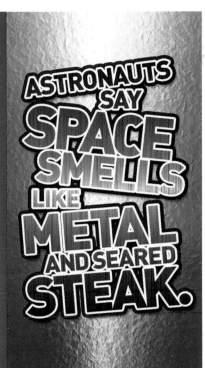

ASTRONAUTS SAY SPACE SMELLS LIKE METAL AND SEARED STEAK.

PREHISTORIC SNAKES, CALLED TITANOBOAS, GREW AS LONG AS SCHOOL BUSES.

RHINO HORNS ARE MADE OF THE SAME SUBSTANCE AS HUMAN FINGERNAILS.

IT'S CONSIDERED →**RUDE**← TO WRITE IN RED INK IN PORTUGAL.

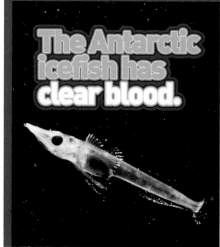

The Antarctic icefish has clear blood.

IN 1960,
A MAN
PARACHUTED
FROM

19.5 MILES
(31.38 km) ABOVE
EARTH—

THAT'S THREE
TIMES AS HIGH
AS COMMERCIAL
AIRLINES FLY.

A LEMUR

CAN WEIGH AS LITTLE AS **FIVE QUARTERS** OR AS MUCH AS A **CAR TIRE,** DEPENDING ON THE SPECIES.

CANADA PRODUCED ENOUGH **MAPLE SYRUP** IN ONE YEAR TO FILL **13** OLYMPIC-SIZE **POOLS.**

SOME WALLABIES HAVE LIGHT PURPLE FUR.

A SALTWATER CROCODILE MAY KEEP ITS MOUTH OPEN TO HELP ITS **BRAIN STAY COOL.**

IN THAILAND, PEOPLE HAVE WATER FIGHTS TO CELEBRATE NEW YEAR'S.

IT TAKES **65** TONS (59 metric tons) **OF PAINT TO COVER THE EIFFEL TOWER.**

A shoe company made a **sneaker** with built-in **screens** that **displayed** social media messages.

THE FLAP OF SKIN UNDER A **MOOSE'S THROAT** IS CALLED **A BELL.**

There was **no ice** in Antarctica

55 million years ago.

IN SINGAPORE, PEOPLE WERE ONCE *FINED* **FOR NOT FLUSHING PUBLIC TOILETS.**

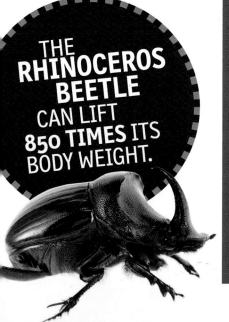

THE **RHINOCEROS BEETLE** CAN LIFT **850 TIMES** ITS BODY WEIGHT.

Ancient **Maya warriors** hurled containers full of **hornets** at enemies.

THE BODY
WEIGHT OF A
SUNFISH
INCREASES

60
MILLION
TIMES
IN ITS LIFETIME.

(AT THAT RATE,
A HUMAN WOULD
GROW TO WEIGH
AS MUCH AS
FOUR *TITANIC*
CRUISE SHIPS!)

A **KOMODO DRAGON** CAN SWALLOW A GOAT WHOLE.

There's a **90 percent** chance your **parents** will **steal** some of your **Halloween candy.**

SCIENTISTS HAVE RETRIEVED **800,000-YEAR-OLD ICE** FROM A **GLACIER** IN ANTARCTICA.

A POPULAR SOFT DRINK IN THE UNITED KINGDOM IS MADE WITH DANDELIONS.

SOME
BAOBAB
TREES
IN AFRICA
ARE MORE THAN
2,000
YEARS OLD.

ATLANTIC HERRING

SOMETIMES FORM SCHOOLS THE SIZE OF NEW YORK CITY.

YOU CAN FIND MORE THAN **1,000 ANCIENT DINOSAUR** AND REPTILE FOOTPRINTS ALONG THE **"DINOSAUR FREEWAY"** — STRETCHING FROM COLORADO TO NEW MEXICO, U.S.A.

A half-inch-long **flatworm** has **60 eyes.** (1.3-cm)

THERE'S A **RADISH** THAT LOOKS LIKE A **WATERMELON** ON THE INSIDE.

A GUENON MONKEY'S WARNING CALL SOUNDS LIKE A LOUD SNEEZE.

145

THE HUMAN BODY CONTAINS A TINY AMOUNT OF GOLD.

A home run in baseball is also called a **"tater."**

DETROIT RED WINGS HOCKEY FANS SOMETIMES **THROW DEAD OCTOPUSES** ONTO THE ICE RINK **TO CELEBRATE A WIN.**

EARTH ONCE SPUN 0.1 MILLISECOND FASTER EACH DAY FOR TWO WEEKS.

A REINDEER'S NOSE HEATS UP AIR ON THE WAY TO THE LUNGS.

AN 18-HOLE GOLF COURSE LIES BETWEEN TWO RUNWAYS AT AN AIRPORT IN ASIA.

ROASTED ANTS ARE A POPULAR SNACK IN COLOMBIA.

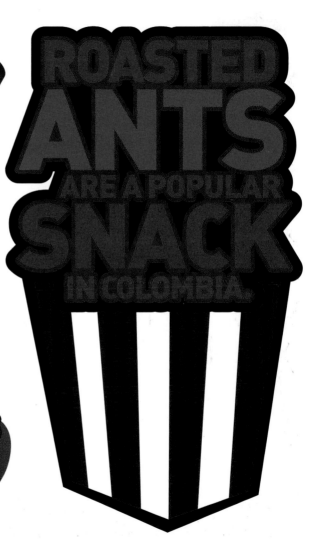

PEOPLE CREATE **HUMAN TOWERS** UP TO **THREE STORIES TALL** AT FESTIVALS IN SPAIN.

When you're driving on the highway, the **car engine** is **hot** enough to **cook** a piece of **chicken.**

There's an annual beauty pageant for camels in the United Arab Emirates, a country in Asia.

A **sloth** can take one week to **digest food.**

The number **4** is considered unlucky in China.

A 25,000-YEAR-OLD FOOTPRINT WAS FOUND IN A FRENCH CAVE.

Strawberries *are members of the* **rose family.**

A TYPICAL AMERICAN **GROCERY STORE** IS STOCKED WITH ABOUT **50,000 ITEMS.**

A REDWOOD TREE CAN PRODUCE UP TO **100,000** SEEDS IN A YEAR.

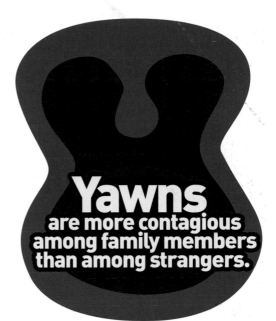

Yawns are more contagious among family members than among strangers.

Some **70 million** years ago, **a rodentlike creature** the size of a rabbit was the largest mammal on Earth.

153

Elephant seals can stay underwater for up to **two hours.**

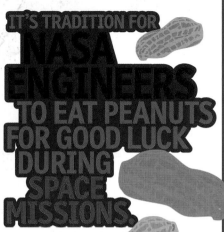

IT'S TRADITION FOR **NASA ENGINEERS** TO EAT PEANUTS FOR GOOD LUCK DURING SPACE MISSIONS.

THE AVERAGE **HOME** PRODUCES MORE AIR POLLUTION THAN A **CAR.**

There are about **14 million** fake **Facebook** accounts.

A STUDY FOUND THAT THE **SOUND OF A KNIFE SCRAPING A BOTTLE** IS ONE OF THE MOST UNPLEASANT SOUNDS IN THE **WORLD.**

AN **ALBATROSS** CAN **GLIDE** THOUSANDS OF MILES **WITHOUT** FLAPPING ITS **WINGS.**

YOU CAN WATCH A MOVIE IN A GRAVEYARD AT THE CINESPIA THEATER IN CALIFORNIA, U.S.A.

Production of Hershey's Kisses was halted during World War II because the foil used to wrap them was rationed.

In Bulgaria and Greece, nodding your head up and down means "no."

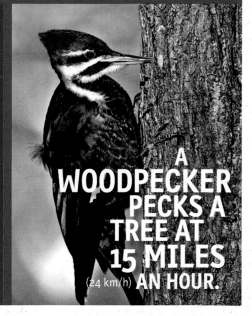

A WOODPECKER PECKS A TREE AT 15 MILES (24 km/h) AN HOUR.

DOGS HAVE THREE TIMES MORE

TASTE
BUDS
THAN CATS.

YOUR **BRAIN** REMEMBERS **10,000 SCENTS.**

IT'S POSSIBLE FOR YOU TO **SPOT THE LIGHT OF A CANDLE** FROM 14 MILES AWAY. (23 km)

CHILDREN'S **HEARING** IS MORE **SENSITIVE** THAN ADULTS'.

YOUR **STOMACH** CAN EXPAND TO **40 TIMES** ITS SIZE.

THE **SKIN** ON YOUR HANDS IS THICKER THAN **15 SHEETS** OF PAPER.

YOUR BODY CAN DETECT **TASTE** IN JUST **.0015 SECOND**— THAT'S AS FAST AS A BLINK OF AN EYE.

YOU HAVE ABOUT **17,000 TOUCH RECEPTORS** IN EACH OF YOUR HANDS.

ON A TV CHANNEL IN NORWAY, a reindeer migration was shown nonstop in real time for **168 HOURS.**

A cabin in NORTH CAROLINA, U.S.A., is covered in 25,000 coffee mugs.

HORSETAIL FALL, in California, U.S.A., is sometimes lit up by the sun, giving it the nickname "FIREFALL."

FRUGIVORE = an animal that eats only (or mostly) fruit

Some WILD PIGS eat SNAKES.

A rough-skinned **NEWT** can survive being **EATEN BY A FROG.**

Nearly all of JAPAN'S cities and towns have a UNIQUE manhole-cover design.

The SCIENTIFIC STUDY of PASSING GAS is called FLATOLOGY.

The average **BRITISH GARDEN** has more than **20,000** SLUGS.

A female **OCTOPUS** can lay **56,000** EGGS.

An American designer CREATED **HIGH HEELS** that look like **ICE SKATES.**

SCIENTISTS made ARTIFICIAL SUNLIGHT that was **10,000** **TIMES STRONGER** than NATURAL SUNLIGHT.

That's Weird!

When explorer **Marco Polo** first saw a **rhinoceros,** he thought it was a **UNICORN.**

165

BUBBLEGUM CORAL IS BRIGHT PINK AND CAN GROW TALLER THAN A TWO-STORY BUILDING.

PEOPLE LIVING ON **PENTECOST ISLAND** IN THE SOUTH PACIFIC HAVE BEEN USING **VINES** TO **BUNGEE JUMP** FOR **1,500** YEARS.

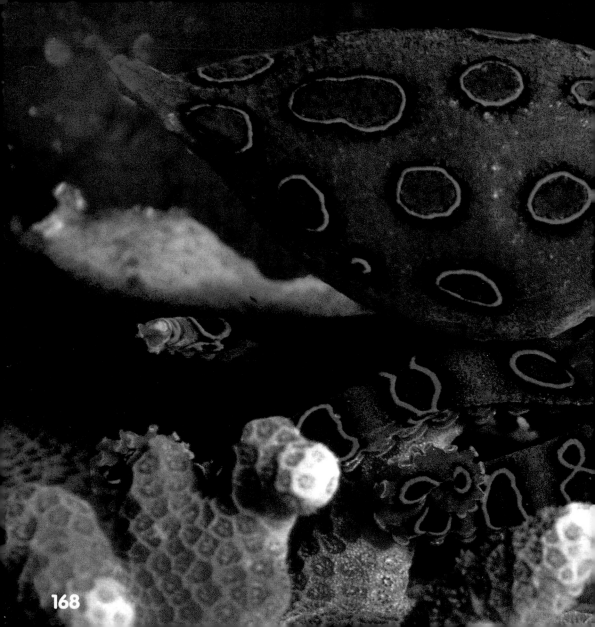

BLUE-RINGED
OCTOPUSES
CAN POISON HUMANS.

Alpaca moms **hum** to comfort their babies.

Swiflet birds' nests are made entirely from saliva.

THE AVERAGE **AMERICAN** GENERATES MORE THAN **FOUR POUNDS** OF **GARBAGE** (1.8 kg) EACH DAY.

Canned **tuna** is one of the most popular **pizza** toppings in Germany.

SOME ANTS CAN WALK UPSIDE DOWN.

Gelada monkey calls sound like a person saying "yep, yep, yep."

THERE'S A PLACE IN VENEZUELA, SOUTH AMERICA, WHERE LIGHTNING FLASHES UP TO 280 TIMES AN HOUR.

FLAMINGOS DON'T TURN PINK UNTIL THEY ARE ABOUT TWO YEARS OLD.

The **Mississippi River** sometimes flows **backward** during powerful hurricanes.

The **iPod's name** was inspired by this line from the classic movie *2001: A Space Odyssey*: **"Open the pod bay doors."**

SNAKES DO NOT HAVE EYELIDS.

Nepal is the only country in the world that doesn't have a rectangular **flag.**

THERE'S A BEACH IN HAWAII WITH GREEN SAND.

SOME TAPEWORMS CAN GROW TO BE 40 FEET LONG (12 m) INSIDE HUMAN INTESTINES.

Some **75,000** (34,019 kg) pounds of meat sank on the R.M.S. *Titanic.*

Yak hair *was used to make* **wigs for** *characters in* **The Hobbit** *movies.*

HALF OF THE PIGS IN THE WORLD LIVE IN CHINA.

A MALL IN THE DESERT CITY OF DUBAI, UNITED ARAB EMIRATES, MAKES SNOW FOR AN INDOOR SKI RESORT.

*The word "**robot**" first appeared in a play written in 1929.*

THE AVERAGE ADULT TELLS ABOUT 11 LIES IN A WEEK.

There's a forest of crooked trees in Poland.

A CANDY COMPANY MADE A CHOCOLATE LOLLIPOP THAT WEIGHED 7,003 POUNDS— (3,176.5 kg) AS MUCH AS A HIPPO!

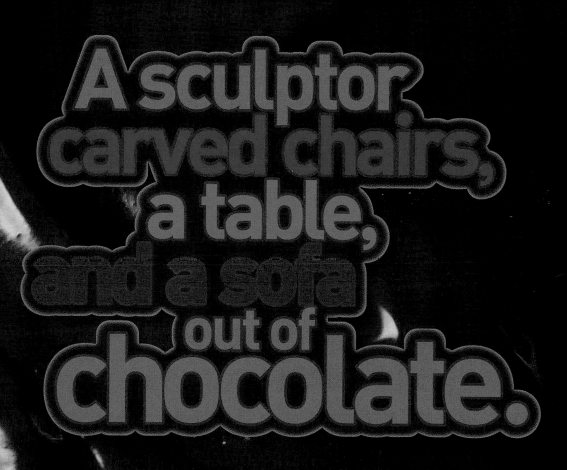

A sculptor carved chairs, a table, and a sofa out of chocolate.

New
York City
**Marathon
runners**
consumed a total of
4,500 pounds
(2,041 kg)
of elbow macaroni
at an annual marathon
eve dinner.

184

THE 1938 COMIC BOOK **IN WHICH** SUPERMAN FIRST APPEARED **SOLD FOR** $2.16 MILLION **IN 2011.**

SPACE JUNK:

MAN-MADE DEBRIS FROM SPACE

FALLS TO EARTH NEARLY EVERY WEEK.

Two people separated by **600 miles** (966 km) *can see the same* **shooting star.**

TRAINED OPERA SINGERS CAN REACH NOTES ALMOST AS LOUD AS A JACKHAMMER.

The most popular password on the Internet is "123456."

THE **PINOCCHIO FROG** IS NAMED FOR ITS **NOSE** THAT CAN INFLATE AND GET **POINTIER.**

ELEPHANTS CAN HEAR EACH OTHER TRUMPET UP TO FIVE MILES (8 km) AWAY.

THERE'S AN ARTIST WHO CREATES TINY PORTRAITS ON HIS FINGERS.

THE "EVERGLADES PIZZA," SOLD IN A FLORIDA, U.S.A., TOWN, IS TOPPED WITH FROG LEGS, ALLIGATOR, AND PYTHON FILLET!

ONE IN THREE PEOPLE SNEEZE AFTER LOOKING AT THE SUN.

SOME SAUROPOD DINOSAURS' NECKS WERE SIX TIMES LONGER THAN A GIRAFFE'S.

HOT-AIR **BALLOONING** WAS ONCE AN OLYMPIC SPORT.

A Chinese student designed a postcard that can capture the smell of your favorite food.

THE POPULAR TEXT MESSAGE ABBREVIATION "OMG," FOR "OH MY GOD," APPEARED NEARLY 100 YEARS AGO IN A LETTER FROM A BRITISH ADMIRAL.

Early jack-o'-lanterns were carved from turnips, potatoes, and beets.

There are seven quintillion, five hundred quadrillion grains of sand on Earth.

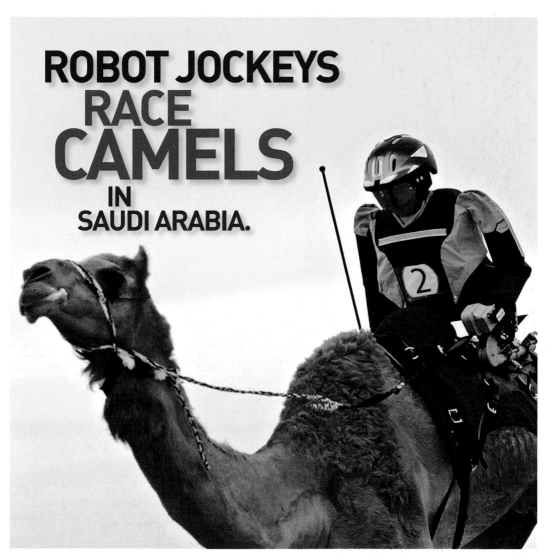

ROBOT JOCKEYS
RACE
CAMELS
IN
SAUDI ARABIA.

THE WORLD'S TINIEST GUITAR IS SMALLER THAN A SPECK OF DUST.

IF ALL OF THE **DNA** IN YOUR **BODY** WAS LINED UP, IT COULD **STRETCH** FROM **PLUTO** TO THE **SUN** AND **BACK.**

Google was originally called BackRub.

A man made a **bike** almost entirely out of **cardboard.**

A CAT NAMED TUXEDO STAN RAN FOR MAYOR OF HALIFAX, NOVA SCOTIA, IN CANADA.

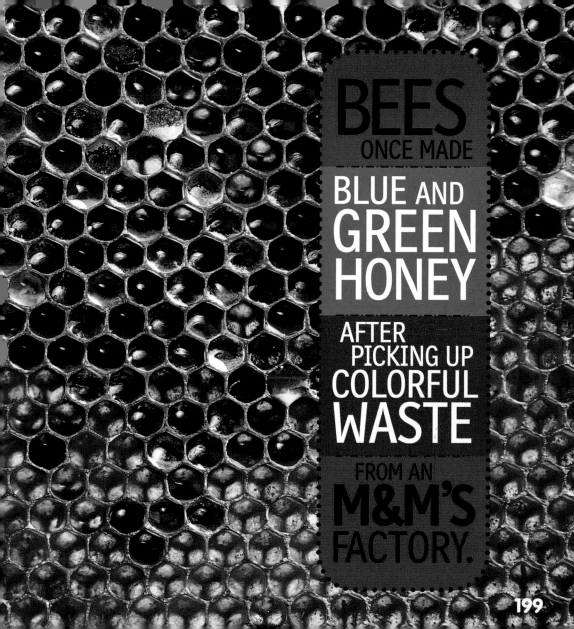

BEES
ONCE MADE
BLUE AND
GREEN
HONEY
AFTER
PICKING UP
COLORFUL
WASTE
FROM AN
M&M'S
FACTORY.

THERE'S ENOUGH ENERGY IN

ONE GALLON
(3.8 L) OF GAS TO CHARGE AN

iPHONE FOR 20 YEARS.

A pumpkin has been chucked more than a mile by a cannon—(1.6 km) a world "punkin' chunkin" record!

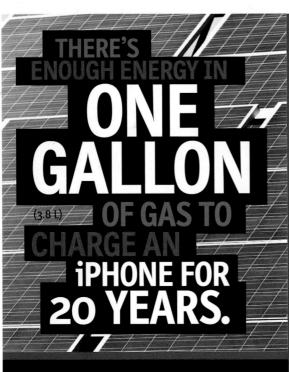

The planet **Uranus** was almost named George.

A **restaurant** filled an aboveground **swimming pool** with more than **13,780 pounds** (6,251 kg) of **pasta.**

There are more vending machines **in Japan** than there are people in New Zealand.

ONLY 0.1 PERCENT OF BACTERIA ACTUALLY MAKE YOU SICK.

Less than **2 percent** *of the world's population has* natural *red hair.*

WHALE WASTE IS AN INGREDIENT IN SOME EXPENSIVE PERFUMES.

You're **more sensitive** to SMELLS when **you're hungry.**

CAPTAIN CRUNCH'S FULL NAME IS HORATIO MAGELLAN CRUNCH.

The sky above the **moon** is always black.

Lady Gaga has a group of ferns named after her.

A MAN SNOWBOARDED ABOUT 17,500 FEET (5,334 m) DOWN MOUNT EVEREST.

Squirrels **sweat** through their **feet.**

Yuma, Arizona, is the **sunniest place** in the United States.

Grass looks greener to girls than it does to boys.

The U.S. president's plane, **Air Force One,** has never landed more than **three seconds off** its scheduled **arrival time.**

207

GUESS WHAT?

Some dogs are really sick of cats!

Hot chocolate tastes sweeter if you _____ !

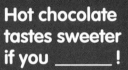

You make **BORBORYGMI** almost every day!

WANNA FIND OUT?

The FUN doesn't have to end here! Find these far-out facts and more in *Weird But True! 6.*

NATIONAL GEOGRAPHIC
Weird but true! 6
350 OUTRAGEOUS FACTS

FACTFINDER

Boldface indicates illustrations.

FACTFINDER

FACTFINDER

PHOTO CREDITS

DS = Dreamstime; GI = Getty Images; MP = Minden Pictures; SS = Shutterstock

Cover and spine (hamster), Subbotina Anna/SS; 2, Subbotina Anna/SS; 4-5, Franco Tempesta; 6, California Skateparks/Solent News; 9 (BACK), Alexandr Makarov/SS; 9, fotomak/SS; 10-11, Frans Lanting/National Geographic Creative; 16-17, cbpix cbpix/iStockphoto; 18, Piyoros C/SS; 20, Anne Saarinen/Alamy; 22-23, Dr. Hendrik Freitag/Department of Biological Sciences, National University of Singapore: The Raffles Bulletin of Zoology 60: pp.37-55; 25, Jack Sullivan/Alamy; 26, ra-photos/iStockphoto; 27, Jackiso/SS; 28-29, Kyodo/Reuters; 30, Franco Tempesta; 32, Greg Wood/AFP/GI; 34-35, Katie Greene/MTC/Newscom; 36, Claudio Contreras/NPL/MP; 38 (BACK), Kelley Tibble/DS; 38 (football player), PCN Photograph/Alamy; 38 (gummy bear), Westend61 GmbH/Alamy; 39, NASA; 40-41, Marilyn Barbone/SS; 41 (space shuttle), NASA; 42, Liz Rubert Pugh; 43, Martin Almqvist/Alamy Stock Photo; 44 (UP), Digital Storm/SS; 44 (LO LE), Brigitte Merle/GI; 44 (LO CTR), AP Photo/Evan Vucci; 44 (LO RT), Museum of Flight Foundation/GI; 45 (UP LE), Ian Schofield/SS; 45 (UP RT), Gordon Sermek/SS; 45 (LO RT), Aaron Amat/SS; 46, Rachael Hamm-Plett; 47, BIG-Bjarke Ingels Group; 48-49, Mike Theiss/National Geographic Creative; 50, CBE/ZOB/WENN.com/Newscom; 51, Dante Fenolio/Photo Researchers RM/GI; 52, Ruth Regina/Wiggles Dog Wigs; 53, Kobby Dagan/SS; 54-55, Eric Isselee/SS; 56, Hugh Lansdown/SS; 59 (perfume bottle), Sebastian_K/Alamy; 60-61, D. Hurst/Alamy; 60-61, Danielle Gali/SuperStock; 62, Tony Wu/MP; 65, ZSSD/MP/National Geographic Creative; 66, craftvision/iStockphoto; 70, lena Brozova/SS; 72-73, Vacclav/SS; 74, AP Images/Franklin eyes; 77, Kjersti Joergensen/SS; 80, Cathy Keifer/SS; 81, urt_G/SS; 83, Bill Greenblatt UPI Photo Service/Newscom; 84 (UP LE), NASA; 84 (UP CTR), Joel Sartore/National Geographic eative; 84 (UP RT), Sergiu Ungureanu/SS; 84 (LO), NatUlrich/S; 85 (UP), AP Photo/Joe Giddens/PA Wire; 85, AP Photo/ ji Sasahara; 87, David Evison/iStockphoto; 90, Joel Sartore/ ational Geographic Creative; 92-93, NASA; 93 (UP), pictafolio/ tockphoto; 94, Eric Isselee/SS; 95, Redmich/iStockphoto; 6 (UP LE), G. Aunion Juan/Alamy Stock Photo; 96 (UP RT), atong/SS; 98, Cathy Keifer/SS; 100, Ashway/Alamy; 102, ebecca Hale, NGP; 102 (BACK), joshlaverty/iStockphoto; 103, ttmann/Corbis/GI; 104-105, Pete Oxford/naturepl.com; 108, rth Wind Picture Archives/Alamy; 110 (LE), Erik Lam/SS; 110 T), GlobalP/iStockphoto; 111, JohnnyMad/iStockphoto; 112 P), subjug/iStockphoto; 112 (LO), Bernd Rohrschneider/MP; 3 (UP), Jonson/DS; 113 (LO), La Petite Maison; 114 (LE), Earth ences and Image Analysis Laboratory, NASA Johnson Space nter; 114 (RT), Sean Pavone/DS; 115, Dave Watts/Alamy;

116-117, Ralph Lee Hopkins/National Geographic Creative; 119 (UP), Cultnat, Dist. RMN-GP/Art Resource, NY; 119 (LO), Woods Hole Oceanographic Institution/Visuals Unlimited, Inc.; 121, NASA/World History Archive & ARPL/Alamy Stock Photo; 122-123, Sandro L. Ramos/SS; 124 (UP LE), Dominick Reuter/GI; 124 (UP CTR), gillmar/SS; 124 (UP RT), Serhiy Smirnov/SS; 124 (LO LE), Yavuz Sariyildiz/SS; 124 (LO RT), DVARG/SS; 125 (UP), Irena Misevic/SS; 125 (LO), Photok.dk/SS; 126 (LE), Janks/DS; 126 (RT), Exactostock/SuperStock; 128 (LE), Jason Prince/SS; 128 (RT), Flip Nicklen/MP; 129, U.S. Air Force; 130, Mark Thiessen; 131, Arto Hakola/SS; 132, D. Hurst/Alamy; 134, Arnold John Labrentz/SS; 135, arlindo71/iStockphoto; 136-137, WaterFrame/Alamy; 138, Jakgree/DS; 139, traveler1116/iStockphoto; 140, Irochka/DS; 141, Ulrich Doering/Alamy; 142-143, Franco Banfi/Waterframe Rm/GI; 144 (UP), Tom Uhlman/Alamy Stock Photo; 144 (LO), Spencer Weiner/GI; 145, worldswildlife-wonders/SS; 148-149, Albert Gea/Reuters; 150, WilleeCole/SS; 151, AlasdairJames/iStockphoto; 153, JFTringali/iStockphoto; 154-155, John Eascott and Yva Momtiuk/National Geographic Creative; 157, Iakov Kalinin/SS; 159, Gerald Marella/SS; 160, GlobalP/iStockphoto; 161, drbimages/iStockphoto; 162-163, Derek Latta/iStockphoto; 164 (UP LE), Iakov Filimonov/SS; 164 (UP CTR), smartdesign91/SS; 164 (UP RT), Phitha Tanpairoj/SS; 164 (LO LE), Keren Su/GI; 164 (LO RT), MriMan/SS; 165 (UP LE), Lisa S./SS; 165 (UP RT), Dave Fleetham/GI; 165 (CTR LE), Estrop/GI; 165 (LO RT), gualtiero boffi/SS; 166, Universal History Archive/GI; 167, KathyGold/SS; 168-169, Richard Merritt FRPS/GI; 170, Juniors Bildarchiv GmbH/Alamy; 171, yingxiaoming/iStockphoto; 172, guenterguni/iStockphoto; 173, Rigoulet Gilles/SuperStock; 174-175, Sunset Boulevard/Corbis/GI; 174-175 (INSET), drfelice/SS; 176, Microstock Man/SS; 177, Eric Isselee/SS; 178 (LE), Thomas Vogel/SS; 178 (RT), Thomas Northcut/SuperStock; 180-181, seawhisper/SS; 182-183, Subbotina Anna/SS; 184, Frank L Junior/SS; 186-187, NASA; 188, Tim Laman/National Geographic Creative; 189, EdStock/iStockphoto; 190, Dito Von Tease; 191, Franco Tempesta; 192-193, sjlayne/iStockphoto; 194 (LE), lucentius/iStockphoto; 194 (CTR), Devonyu/iStockphoto; 194 (RT), Buriy/iStockphoto; 195, AP Images/Kamran Jebreili; 196, Kriangkrai Wangjai/SS; 197, Hugh Chisholm; 198-199, Vincent Kessler/Reuters; 200, ithinksky/iStockphoto; 201, LindaYolanda/iStockphoto; 202, Artens/SS; 203, Patrik Mezirka/SS; 204-205, jannoon028/SS; 204 (sun), Cammeraydave/DS; 204 (sunglasses), Marilyn Gould/DS; v206-207, U.S. Air Force

Since 1888, the National Geographic Society has
funded more than 12,000 research, exploration,
and preservation projects around the world.
The Society receives funds from National
Geographic Partners, LLC, funded in part by
your purchase. A portion of the proceeds from
this book supports this vital work. To learn
more, visit natgeo.com/info.

For more information, visit
nationalgeographic.com, call 1-800-647-5463,
or write to the following address:

National Geographic Partners
1145 17th Street N.W.
Washington, D.C. 20036-4688 U.S.A.

Visit us online at nationalgeographic.com/books

For librarians and teachers:
ngchildrensbooks.org

More for kids from National Geographic:
natgeokids.com

For information about special discounts
for bulk purchases, please contact National
Geographic Books Special Sales:
specialsales@natgeo.com

For rights or permissions inquiries, please
contact National Geographic Books Subsidiary
Rights: bookrights@natgeo.com

Designed by Rachael Hamm Plett, Moduza Design

First edition published 2013
Reissued and updated 2018

Trade paperback: 978-1-4263-3112-1
Reinforced library binding ISBN:
978-1-4263-3113-8

The publisher would like to thank Jen Agresta,
project manager; Sarah Wassner Flynn, project
manager; Julie Beer, researcher; Michelle
Harris, researcher; Robin Terry, project
editor; Paige Towler, project editor; Eva
Absher-Schantz, art director; Julide Dengel,
art director; Kathryn Robbins, art director;
Ruthie Thompson, designer; Lori Epstein, ph
director; Hillary Leo, photo editor; Molly Reid,
production editor; and Anne LeongSon and
Gus Tello, production assistants.

Printed in China
18/PPS/2